MW01533101

BITCHCRAFT:
SPELLS FROM A WICKED WITCH'S GRIMOIRE

Lady Katerina

Table of Contents

Note from Katerina

I have been an active practitioner of magick since 2003, a little around 15 years…things in this book may not be new to people who have been practicing longer, but some may be unheard of concepts. I hope that you take at least one thing away when you read this, I don't care if it is the most irrelevant thing, I just want you to learn something. xoxox

This book is a collection of spells, tricks, curses, and the such that I have came across in my time as a practitioner of magick. These range from being Wiccan based spells, Voodoo rituals, Santeria spells, and Hoodoo tricks. I identify as a witch. I have no set beliefs and practices as I switch from one to another— whatever suits my needs for whatever situation. Do not call me a Wiccan as I do not adhere to the threefold law or the Wiccan Rede…sometimes a curse is necessary and people will get hurt. I do not believe that any workings I do will return upon me times three…I do believe in Karma however, but I feel like it will not take effect until the next lifetime, or never…as I said sometimes people deserve to be cursed!

You should know some basics before partaking in any spells in this book, you need to know substitutions for herbs, color coordination, and days of the weeks…and phases of the moon. Days of the week and the phases of the moon are not really important, but they do help when you are casting, to make the magick more potent. So to start off I will tell you what days are best for what, then moon phases, then colors, and then herbs. I hope you enjoy this and get something useful out of this book.

Also it should be noted that I am not a wicked witch…I just don't take shit from anyone, which some may feel makes me a bitch…fuck 'em!

Much Luck,

Lady Katerina

Days of The Week & Their Correspondences

Monday

Perform spells and rituals involving agriculture, animals, fertility, reconciliation, theft, voyages, dreams, emotions, clairvoyance, home, family, medicine, cooking, purity, truth, travel, personality, merchandising, psychic work, Faerie magic, and the Goddess.

Tuesday

Perform spells and rituals involving force, power, war, protection, energy, endurance, passion, sex, courage, aggression, courage, physical strength, guns, tools, confrontation, repairs, machinery, revenge, surgery, breaking negative spells, enemies, prison, hunting, politics, contests, victory, and athletics.

Wednesday

Perform spells and rituals involving the conscious mind, study, travel, divination, wisdom, communication, and luck.

Thursday

Perform spells and rituals involving optimism, growth, physical well-being, good health, material success, expansion, money, wealth, prosperity, leadership, generosity, happiness, siblings, neighbors, contracts, legal matters, fertility, riches, clothing, money, desires, business, group pursuits, joy, laughter, expansion, writing, knowledge, teaching, intellectual pursuits, reasoning, logic, skill, self-improvement, debt, fear, loss, and flexibility.

Friday

Perform spells and rituals involving love, romance, courtship, dating, friendship, luxury, income, reconciliation, beauty, relationships disputes, desirability, marriage, sexual matters, partnerships, social activities, strangers, pleasure, music, nature, arts, and crafts.

Saturday

Perform spells and rituals involving longevity, exorcism, endings, death, karma, apprehension, austerity, caution, stalkers, limitations, habit breaking, scientific experimentation, restriction, spirit, communication, meditation, psychic attack or defense, finding lost items, wills, locating a missing person, self-discipline, freedom, diseases, removing pests, and boundaries.

Sunday

Perform spells and rituals involving the ego, careers, goals, healing, spirituality, strength, fatherhood, politics, individuality, hope, fortune, work, power, promotions, strength, and spirituality.

It is important to note that not all traditions of magick follow this, in fact some ignore days of the week entirely. Its entirely up to you. I cannot stress this enough but, your intentions and desires are all that truly matter in the end.

Moon Phases

New Moon

The new moon is the beginning of the lunar cycle, and means that the moon is completely in line with the sun and the earth. We see a dark sky with no visible moon. It's a time of newness and rejuvenation. The new moon is the three days after the new face of the moon and also includes the day of the new face of the moon.

Spells

New beginnings of any sort, beauty, health, personal improvement or new employment.

Waxing Moon

The waxing moon is the period of time between the new moon and the full moon. Every night, the moon gets a little larger. Any spellwork that requires growth should be done now.

Spells

Courage, motivation, inspiration, friendship, elemental magick, healing or luck.

Full Moon

This is a time when the Moon is at its most powerful, and the magic most potent. Performing any positive spell at this time will achieve good results. Since the full moon only truly occurs for one night out of the entire lunar cycle, it can be hard to fit it into your schedule. You can harness the energy of the full moon for about 2 days before or after the night the moon is truly full.

Spells

Artistic projects, love, romance, fertility, psychic abilities or making decisions. Also healing, guidance, and completion spells.

Waning Moon

The moon is waning as it gets smaller again, after the full moon. As the moon seems to disappear in the sky, use this time to do spellwork to remove things from your life. The waning moon is a good time for the casting out of the old ways, banishing old habits such as smoking and overeating, the removal of troubles and worries.

Spells

Banishing bad habits and addictions, ending relationships, banishing stalkers or bad people from your life.

Dark of the Moon / Dark Moon

The Dark of the Moon (or Dark Moon) is traditionally the last three days of the Lunar cycle, immediately preceding the New Moon, and the time when the night sky is notably absent the presence of the Moon. The dark time is a time of retreat, healing, and dreaming of the future.

Spells

Healing, renewal, psychic spells. A good time to meditate on the inner self.

Colors

Black
Grounding, wisdom, learning, protection, safety, reversing, uncrossing, unhexing, hexing, crossing, cursing, banishing negativity, repelling black magick, scrying, pride.

Blue
House blessing, animal/pet magick, earth magick, concentration, material goods, stability, locating lost objects, earth element, real estate, construction, food, financial crisis.

Gold
Masculine divinity, great fortune, abundance, prosperity, male energy, understanding, divination, fast luck, solar/sun energy, positive attitude, justice, health, attraction, luxury.

Gray
Loneliness, glamour, contemplation, removing negative influence.

Green
Prosperity, abundance, money, physical & emotional healing, growth, luck, marriage, tree/plant magick, acceptance, weather, counteract envy/greed/jealousy.

Orange
Creativity, self- expression, intellectual matters, overcoming addiction, legal matters/justice, joy, business success, ambition, vitality, fun, action, opportunity, celebration, investments.

Pink
Love, compassion, nurturing, femininity, friendship, romance, partnership, spiritual & emotional healing, protection of children, domestic harmony, self- improvement, maturity.

Purple
Wisdom, influence, spiritual power, contact with spirits, drive away evil, change luck, independence, government, break habits.

Red
Passion, vitality, strength, survival, fertility, courage, sexual potency, mercy, action, danger, war, fire element, conflict, sports, independence, assertiveness, competition.

Yellow
Pleasure, success, happiness, learning, memory, concentration, persuasion, inspiration, imagination, solar magick, charm, confidence, air element, travel, flexibility

White
All purpose, unity, purity, cleansing, peace, balance, spirituality, healing, innocence, rain, magick involving young children, truth, consecration, balancing the aura.

White can be used to substitute any color.

Colors for Black Magick

BLACK

Black is an all-purpose color and when available, black should be used with other colors in every ritual. Different colors attract different energies and stimulate certain vibrations in the chakras. Using candles of specific colors can help to amplify the energies in ritual and spell work. Black candles used in workings of destruction are used to incite the slower destruction of enemies, opposed to accidents or sudden attacks associated with the color red. Black is also a good color to use to bring discord and confusion to enemies. Black absorbs, conceals, creates confusion and chaos, is used for new beginnings, and obtaining knowledge of hidden things. Black is the container of light, and is one of the most powerful of colors. Saturn rules black. Black influences self-control, endurance, and patience. Spells using black energy are best performed during a waning Moon, on a Saturday when the planet Saturn is strongly placed and waxing.

BLUE

Blue Candles are good to use in spells pertaining to spirituality, meditation, summoning Demons, healing, sincerity, obtaining the truth, influencing fidelity and loyalty, bringing inner peace, and for knowledge and wisdom. Blue can also be used for establishing harmony in the home, for increasing occult power, and for spiritual protection. For workings of black magick, blue can be used for inciting depression, sadness, and hopelessness, lack of sympathy, coldness, and gloom. Jupiter rules royal blue. Workings using blue energy should be done on a Monday or Thursday.

BROWN

Brown Candles can be used for communicating with nature spirits and for grounding and centering one's self. Brown is used in spells for solidity, neutrality, and practicality. In workings of black magick, brown is used for inciting indecision, hesitancy, sadness, dullness, and uncertainty.

GREEN

Green Candles are used in spells for beginnings, growth, abundance, fertility, healing, success, general good luck, harmony, and influencing generosity. Green is used in spells for love, marriage, and making love. Green influences affection, opposed to red, which is used for passionate love, lust, and sex. In workings of black magick, green is used for inciting jealousy, greed, suspicion, resentment, sickness, disease, and disharmony. Venus rules the color green. Workings using green energy should be performed during a waxing moon on a Friday when Venus is strongly placed.

GREY

Grey Candles are used in spells for inducing death, illness, and/or to incite mourning and sadness. Saturn should be strongly placed.

ORANGE

Orange Candles are used for creativity. Orange helps in spells for adaptability, sexual attraction, sexual stimulation, sex magick, enthusiasm, and energy. Orange helps with attraction, sudden changes, energy stimulation, gaining control, changing luck and inciting justice. The Sun rules orange. Workings using orange energy are best performed on a Sunday when the Sun is strongly placed.

RED

Red Candles are used for energy, vitality, inciting passion, arousing anger, pure lust and for physical gratification. Red is inflammatory and is used in spells for revenge, anger, courage, determination, and dealing with enemies. Red can be used for protection against psychic attack and for self-confidence. Red incites accidents, fires, and injuries. It is used in spells to invoke power and intensity before workings of black magick. When used in black magick, red as opposed to black brings on sudden attacks, accidents, bloodshed, violence, and hatred. Red can also be used to incite wars, anarchy, and cruelty. Mars rules red. Workings using the color red should be performed on Tuesdays when Mars is strongly placed and waxing.

PURPLE

Violet/Purple Candles are used for enhancing psychic ability, bringing wisdom, for divination, to remove curses, for healing, business success, and for influencing people in power. For workings of black magick, purple can be used to incite tyranny, abuse of power, and for bringing sadness and treachery to others. Jupiter rules purple. Workings using the color purple should be performed on Thursdays. Workings for psychic power should be performed on Mondays when the Moon is strongly placed and full.

YELLOW

Yellow Candles are used in workings for passing exams, and for increasing one's intelligence and intellect. Yellow energy rules over the logical conscious side of the brain, computers, communication, audio, video, TV, electronics, books, literature and the will. Yellow is used to improve the mind, to deepen concentration, for mental (left-brained power), to enhance learning ability, and for speech, writing, and publishing. Yellow rules over media concerns, gossip, slander, interviews, brothers, sisters, neighbors, rumors, theft, and all areas of study and communication. Yellow is also used to overcome addictions, and to break habits. Yellow is also good for friendship. In workings of black magick, yellow is used to incite infidelity, cowardice, decay, disease, dying, insanity, and inconsistency in others. Mercury rules over the color yellow. Yellow energy is best used on Wednesdays and Sundays. For anything pertaining to intellect and communication, do the working on a Wednesday. For workings using the force of will, these are best performed on a Sunday.

WHITE

White Candles are for cleansing, purity, and innocence. The Moon should be strong. For workings of black magick, white can be used to incite corruption, bring impotence, and to destroy the sex drive. White can also be used to create weakness, neurosis, and fear. The Moon rules white. Workings using white energy should be performed on Monday.

!!Reminder!!
White can be used as a substitute for any color.

Herbal Substitutions

ACACIA= Gum Arabic
ACACIA GUM= Gum Arabic
ACONITE= Tobacco
ARABIC GUM= Frankincense, Gum Mastic, Gum Tragacanth
(for binding wet ingredients, not for incense)
AMMONIAC GUM= Asafetida
ASAFOETIDA= Tobacco; Valerian
BALM OF GILEAD= Rose buds, Gum Mastic
BDELLIUM , GUM= Copal; Pine resin; Dragons Blood
BELLADONNA= Tobacco
BENZOIN= Gum Arabic; Gum Mastic
CACHANA= Angelica Root
CARNATION= Rose petals anointed with a few drops of clove oil
CASSIA= Cinnamon
CASTOR BEAN= A few drops of Castor Oil
CEDAR= Sandalwood
CINQUEFOIL= Clover; Trefoil
CITRON= Equal parts of Orange Peel & Lemon Peel
CLOVE= Mace, Nutmeg
CLOVER= Cinquefoil
COPAL= Frankincense; Cedar
COWBANE= Tobacco
CYPRESS= Juniper; Pine needles
DEERSTONGUE= Tonka Bean (not for internal use); Woodruff; Vanilla
DITTANY OF CRETE= Gum Mastic
DRAGONS BLOOD= Equal Parts of Red Sandalwood and Frankincense
EUCALYPTUS OIL= Camphor oil; Lavender Oil
EUPHORBIUM = Tobacco
FRANKINCENSE= Copal; Pine resin
GALANGAL= Ginger Root
GRAINS OF PARADISE= Black Pepper
GUM AMMONIAC= Asafetida
GUM BDELLIUM= Copal; Pine resin; Dragons Blood
HELLEBORE= Tobacco; Nettle
HEMLOCK = Tobacco
HEMP= Nutmeg; Damiana; Star Anise; Bay
HENBANE= Tobacco
HYSSOP= Lavender
IVY= Cinquefoil
JASMINE= Rose
JUNIPER= Pine
LAVENDER= Rose

LEMONGRASS= Lemon Peel
LEMON PEEL= Lemongrass;
LEMON VERBENA= Lemongrass; Lemon peel
MACE= Nutmeg
MANDRAKE= Tobacco
MASTIC GUM= Gum Arabic; Frankincense
MINT(any sort) = Sage
MISTLETOE= Mint; Sage
MUGWORT= Wormwood
NEROLI OIL= Orange Oil
NIGHTSHADE= Tobacco
NUTMEG= Mace; Cinnamon
OAKMOSS= Patchouli
ORANGE= Tangerine Peel
ORANGE FLOWERS= Orange Peel
PATCHOULI= Oakmoss
PEPPERMINT= Spearmint
PEPPERWORT = Rue; Grains of Paradise; Black Pepper
PINE= Juniper
PINE RESIN= Frankincense; Copal
RED SANDALWOOD= Sandalwood mixed with a pinch of Dragons Blood
ROSE= Yarrow
ROSE GERANIUM = Rose
RUE= Rosemary mixed with a pinch of black pepper
SAFFRON= Orange Peel
SANDALWOOD = Cedar
SARSAPARILLA= Sassafras
SASSAFRAS= Sarsaparilla
SPEARMINT = Peppermint
SULFUR = Tobacco; Club Moss; Asafetida
THYME = Rosemary
TOBACCO= Bay
TONKA BEAN= Vanilla
TREFOIL= Cinquefoil
VALERIAN= Asafetida
VANILLA= Woodruff; Deerstongue; Tonka Bean
VETIVERT= Calamus
WOLFSBANE = Tobacco
WOOD ALOE= Sandalwood Sprinkled with Ambergris Oil
WOODRUFF= Deerstongue; Vanilla
WORMWOOD= Mugwort
YEW = Tobacco

It should be noted that Rosemary can be substituted for any herb. Rose can be substituted for any flower. Frankincense or Copal can be substituted for any gum resin. And Tobacco can be substituted for any poisonous herb.

Items Used in Black Magick

- Black candles.

- Oils; Banishing oil, Hot foot oil, crossing oil

- Herbs; red pepper, wormwood, tobacco, belladonna.

- Your Fluids; Blood, Sexual juices and other body fluids.

- Coffins Nails, broken glass, razor blades, poppets, graveyard dirt, goofer dust, bones, sulfur, coins, jars, dragons blood ink.

Personal Items Of The Victim

If you have none of these, then write the victims name on a piece of paper and if possible their date of birth and any other information you have on them, such as where they live.

- A photo, clothing, hair, fingernail clippings, personal possessions, sexual fluids...even a gift they have given you.

Whatever is readily available to one can be incorporated into one's spells, as with colors and herbs anything can be substituted...and spells can be adjusted so that they fit ones needs.

For example, if doing a jar spell...and you do not have a jar, but have a glass bottle...that can substitute the jar...be creative, what truly matters in any spell is the intent and one's desire for it to be.

Always make sure your substitutions are acceptable substitutions in any spell, you do not want to fuck your spell up by using sweetener in place of graveyard dirt and have the one you were cursing actually develop sweet romantic feelings for you, or vice versa!

BE SMART.

 *Spells*

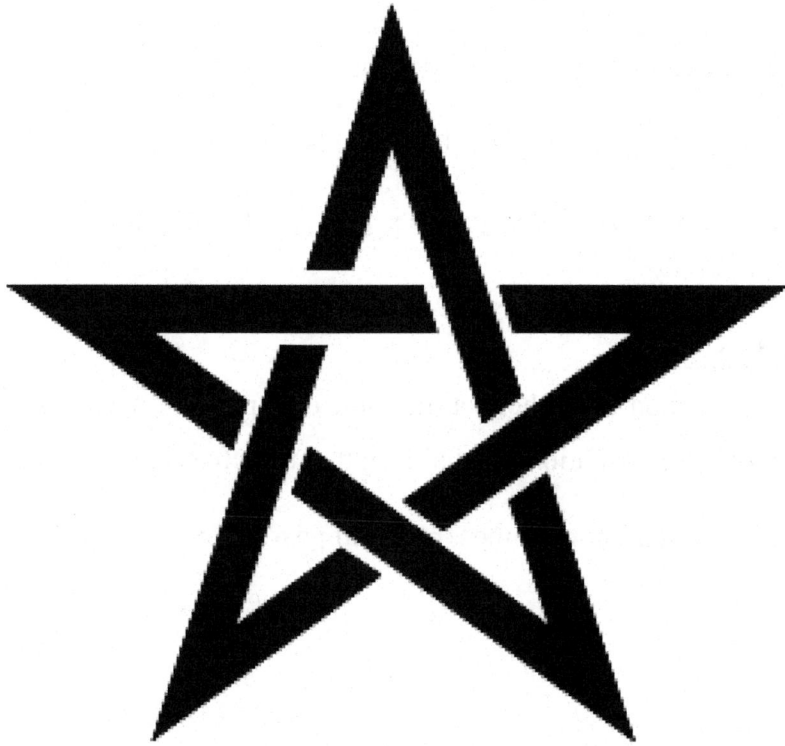

Money Spell

This is a Santeria spell for money. I learned this not too long ago, and the night of doing the spell I went to sleep shortly after, slept maybe 6 hours, if even, and when I awoke I checked my account and I had money I was not expecting, and the two following days after I was finding and getting money from people for no reason…I accumulated about 73 dollars in 3 days. Typically, the spell takes a full week to take full effect but, results can be seen within a few hours. You should only do this spell once a week!

Items Needed
2 white candles
Money (dollar bill, or whatever bill you have handy…just no change!)
Pencil
Cup of coffee (can be instant, hot, iced, etc…as long as it is coffee)

The candles should be placed beside each other, light the candles and place the coffee in the middle (this is for Saint Lazarus) . Grab the money and write on it with the pencil:
"Saint Lazarus blesses the owner of the bill with an abundance of money and bless me too".
fold and hold the bill with both hands and repeat what you wrote 3 times.
Now put the bill in your wallet (if you don't have a wallet put it anywhere you want like in your pillow, under your mattress, just hide it…)
if using chime/spell candles wait until they are consumed (if using a big candle wait about 10-20 minutes and then blow the candles out) and drink some of the coffee, this symbolizes you greeting and letting Lazarus into your life to ensure a quick flow of money, pour the rest of the coffee out onto the earth (the ground). The offer, your coffee, will be accepted once this is done.

Command and Compel Spell

The purpose of this spell is to command someone to love you.

Items Needed
Red pencil and brown paper

Take the piece of brown paper and cut it into a square. Using a red pencil, write the name of your loved one nine times. Turn the paper 90 degrees to the right and write your name over theirs nine times. Fold the paper three times. While doing this, focus intensely on your desires. Repeat the following as you hold the paper to your heart:

> *"I command you, I compel you Love me, as I love you*
>
> *I command you, I compel you, (Name) return to me now!"*

Now, burn the paper and scatter the ashes to the wind.

In 27 days, if you have not heard from your beloved repeat the above actions. You can do this spell every 27 days to strengthen the work.

Love from A Specific Person

The spell is best done at night.

Items Needed
Fireproof container
Piece of white paper
Red and black pen
Herbs to burn (associated with love)

Light a small fire in the container. Cut out a piece of paper that is 3x3 inches.
With the red pen draw a heart on the paper and color it in. Write the name of the person that you desire on the heart three times. While doing this be thinking of his or her heart burning with desire for you just like the flames of the fire. Kiss the names on the heart 3 times. Place the paper in the fire while saying this 3 times:

> *"Soon my love will come to me*
> *This I know that it must be*
> *Fire come from this wood*
> *Bring love and caring that it would*
> *Make our hearts glow and shine,*
> *bringing love that shall be mine!"*

Sit quietly as the paper burns, visualize your lover coming towards you. When you are finished concentrating, extinguish the fire. Then say this quietly three times:

"So, let it be"

Security in a bottle

To protect oneself from enemies, prepare a witch's bottle, this helps protect from known and unknown enemies. You may bury the bottle on your property.

Items Needed

Glass jar with a tight fitting lid
Sharp objects (glass, nails, razors, pins, needles, splinters, etc)
Personal taglock (your hair or fingernail clippings, or blood will do)
Your Urine (semen and menstrual blood are optional)
Tape or wax to seal the jar shut

Fill the jar halfway full with the sharp objects, then add your personal items (taglocks), if you choose to then add the menstrual blood or semen, then finish filling the jar up with your urine. Screw the lid on tight and seal with the tape of wax. If you can bury the bottle a foot deep as close to your front door as possible, but if this is not an option…you can place the jar out of sight, hidden somewhere in the back of your closet or cabinets. It will protect you from anyone who wishes ill upon you.

Money Drawing Ritual

Items Needed

Dollar bills
Permanent marker
Glue stick

Take one or more of one dollar bills and write upon them a blessing with permanent marker: *"May you be blessed with health, wealth and love"*. These are the blessed bucks, grab a glue stick and head out into the world to hide them. NEVER let anyone see you hide them and never drop one to make it look like an accident. This is an intentional spell that only works when it is intentional, it sets into motion "reap what you sow", so that what you give you shall get back 100 fold. You can hide them anywhere, in the grocery store, the mall, glue it to something. The only rule is that you should not ever stay to see who finds the bills.

To Cross an Enemy

Carve the name of one you want to cross in a black cross candle. Turn the candle upside down and carve away at the wax until the wick is exposed from the bottom. Burn upside down. Dispose of the wax remains in a cemetery.

Self Defense Doll Magick

Sew a doll out of black fabric, fill it with organic items...such as leaves, grass, trees, etc. cut a slit in the back and sprinkle pepper into the doll, and write the name of your victim on a piece of paper and slide it into the hole as well. Sew the opening with a piece of wire. Bend the dolls arms backwards and tie its hands together. This ensure the victim is helpless, then finally place the doll in a kneeling position facing the wall (in a corner). This robs them of their vital energies...this should only be justified when your own life is threatened, or the life of a loved one.

Tower Tarot Card Hex

To create chaos and havoc for the target, write their name in black ink across a copy of the tower tarot card...burn it and scatter it to the wind.

Black Coffin Death Spell

This is an old spell, used mainly in the southern United States. A coffin, around 2-3 inches long is made from wood, wax, clay or whatever is easy to make it from. It is painted black. A small doll pierced with pins is placed in it. At night it is placed on thy enemy's doorstep, and a burnt stump of black candle is placed at each end. Some sprinkle an oil such as XX Doublecross oil or Black Art oil on the coffin before placing it.

Paper Hex Ritual

A black piece of paper is cut into the shape of a man or woman of whom you dislike, the paper should be black. Use dove blood red ink to write the person's name on the paper image. Stick a new pin at the head and thread it in and out of the image all the way down to the feet. This will cause the paper to fold up and become small. Place the image and pin in a small box and take it to a cemetery. Dig a small hole and place the box in it, on top of the box sprinkle some devil's shoe string roots and sprinkle the roots and box with black arts oil. Finally cover with dirt from the graveyard, leave the cemetery and never return to where you buried the box.

Full Circle Curse

Hold your right hand up above your head, index finger pointing upward, ad move counter clockwise in a circular motion and say:

> *"I vow before this day is done*
> *before the setting of the sun*
> *that all you say and all you do*
> *will fly directly back at you.*
> *And all that hurt and all that pain*
> *And all the anguish it contains*
> *Shall rain on you like pelting hail*
> *And take you down by forceful gale."*

Conjure Bag To Cross Someone

To cross someone, or bring bad luck a conjure bad is made using 9 new needles, 9 new pins tied together with some hair of the intended victim. To this add a piece of snakeroot, some goofer dust power….put this all into a red flannel bad which is then hidden in the victims home, or buried in their yard. As long as the bad remains unfound the spell will work.

Graveyard Curse

Items Needed
Gift for the dead

Write a letter to the dead one explaining your problem and what you would like done about the situation. Be very precise and thorough with your instructions, do not leave anything out and **DO NOT LEAVE ANY MEASURES UP FOR THE SPIRIT TO DECIDE.**
When done with the letter go to the grave of the deceased, read your letter aloud tell them you have also brought them a gift as payment for their help. Dig a shallow hole where you would imagine their right hand to be, bury the gift and letter in the hole, thank the spirit, and leave the cemetery **AND DO NOT LOOK BACK while leaving!**

Occult Seduction Spell

For this you will need something which has came into contact with the person you wish to seduce…hair and fingernail clippings are best…cigarettes or a tissue they touched is second best. This is called your contact object. On the night of the new moon, wait until you are sure the person of your desire is sleeping. Then sit in a darkened room and hold the contact object, cupped in your hands, against your breast. Close your eyes and quietly say the name of the person you are lusting for and recite:

"Power of lust
Hear my sign,
Naked feel
Your flesh to mine."

You should put your entire heart and soul into this chant…then wrap your contact object in a tissue and hold it in your hands as you retire for the night.
Do this for 7 consecutive nights

Revenge Spell

Get a photograph of your enemy, some salt, some sulfur from an unburnt match (scrape the red tip from the match). Throw some salt upon the photo and say

"As this salt is of the earth,
so art thee.
And as I trod upon the earth,
So do I trod upon thee."

Now sprinkle the sulfur over the photo, around the area of the forehead; light the sulfur so that a hole burns in the forehead region. This will carry your incantation to the subconscious mind of your enemy, and he will create his own downfall. Chant:

"Friends of fire, and friends of hell,
beckon to this horrid smell.
Destroy the empire that he's built,
Let him suffer with his guilt.
From earth's own salt and sulfur's smell,
With your own evil you shall dwell.
With evil thought and vicious tongue,
I will undo what you have done.
No longer will you manipulate,
With your deeds you seal your fate.
The smell of vengeance is so sweet,
With these words my spell's complete."

Say the above with meaning, conjure up as much emotion as you can and keep in mind that whatever your enemy gets, he deserves.

Sigil Curse

For this curse you will write the victims first and last name, their birthday and where they live...if all of the information is not available...the name will do. Write this on a piece of paper and below it draw these symbols :

you will also need salt and a bowl of water.
Now start burning the paper and imagine the little fucker who has done you wrong, imagine their pain and the justice that they will get because of you, while saying:

"this is the image of my would be victim,
it I hand from a single thread
in a place no one shall see.
It will bring fear in the heart of (her/him) who shall harm me,
It will bring fear in the heart of (him/her) who would harm me.
(s/he) will be binded by fear from harming me further.
(s/he) will be binded by fear from harming me at all.
I will tie a knot in the thread when I wish to secure the fear
Until I break it
So mote it be"

When burned throw it into the water, and throw salt in it. Then throw it in the trash.

Freezer Jar Spell

Write the bothersome person's name on a piece of paper, if you can obtain a copy of their signature this would be ideal, but their name will do. Tie the paper up with a red string that has been knotted 9 times, get a small jar... bottle...whatever, a baby food jar will work...make sure it is glass. Stuff the paper in the jar with some garlic, close the lid and seal it with candle wax...white, black or red are good choices. Place the jar in the freezer, in the very very back where no one will find it...within a week the bothersome person should stop bothering you, if not start over with a new jar. Dispose of the previous in running water, such as a river.

Burn It Away Banishing

Items needed: slip of paper, pen, a fireproof bowl, and matches or a lighter.

To begin write down what you are banishing...a person or spirit, a bad habit, etc...focus on what you have written for a moment, call it to mind as clearly as you can. Light the slip of paper on fire and drop it into the bowl. As it burns imagine the target leaving your life and then focus all of your attention on what your life will be like after the banishing takes effect. When the paper is done burning dispose of the ashes away from your house…just get them away from you ASAP!

CURSE OF REVENGE

This curse is to be laid upon the victim while burning an image of the victim (wax sigil, photograph, drawing, anything) in the flame of a consecrated black candle Speak aloud the following:

"There has been unfairness done to me
I summon the elements
I envoke them
I conjure them to do my bidding

The four watchtowers shall lay their eyes and minds
there shall be fear and guilt and bad blood
there shall be submission and no pity

I point the threefold law against thee
against thee it shall be pointed
threefold, a hundred fold,
is the cost for my anger and pain

Thou shalt be blinded by the fear
blinded by the pain
blinded by me
binded by me
Cursed by me
So mote it be!"

Hex to bring Discord and Darkness

You will use thick string or yarn, about 9 or 10 inches long. Tie 3 separate knots while saying:
"With this knot I seal this hex
you will not sleep, you will not rest
Knots of anger, knots of hate
Discord brings you to your fate
I tie this second knot makes two
Bringing darkness over you
Slander, discord, evil too
Bringing darkness straight to you
With this third knot, I do bind
Weaving chaos in your mind
Hex of anger, hex of hate
Bring him down, I will not wait

So mote it be"

As you do this spell think of all the chaos that you will be bring to your enemy. When finished, hide the cord with the knots tied in or around their home to increase its effectiveness.

Bones of Anger Hex

 Gather bones of chickens and dry them in the sun for a few days. Then when you are ready to do this hex make sure you are worked up into a frenzy of anger and hatred. This will add to the potency of your hex! Be thinking of all this while doing this hex and when it says 'With these bones I now do crush" take a hammer or use your feet to stomp and crush these bones as if they were your enemy before you! When you are done sweep them up and place them in a bag. You will then want to sprinkle the dust and remains of the bones on your enemies property around his house. If you have a bell ring it 3 times and say... *"I call upon the Ancient Ones from the great abyss to do my bidding I invoke Cuthalu, God of Anger and the creatures of the underworld hear me now... "Bones of anger, bones to dust full of fury, revenge is just I scatter these bones, these bones of rage take thine enemy, bring him pain I see thine enemy before me now I bind him, crush him, bring him down With these bones I now do crush Make thine enemy turn to dust torment, fire, out of control With this hex I curse your soul. So it be!"*

Three Nights of Hell Candle Spell

This spell is designed to inflict serious pain and sores on thine enemy for a period of three days. After which the spell is lifted and he is made well again.

Take a black candle and place a picture of thine enemy in front of you. Tilt the candle so the wax drips upon the picture. Visualize the wax burning sores into the body of thine enemy. Say three times:

> *"As I do this candle spell*
> *Bring thine enemy three nights of hell*
> *Candle black, black as night*
> *Bring him pains of flesh tonight!*
> *Lesions on his skin will grow*
> *Afflict him with a painful blow*
> *Sores and pain afflict him now*
> *for three nights he'll wonder how*
> *Dukes of darkness, Kins of hell*
> *Smite thine enemy, bring him hell*
> *when three nights of pain have past*
> *Make him well, well at last"*

Empower the sores and pain with mediation and then extinguish the candle. After three nights have past, destroy the picture and say:

> *"When three nights of pain endured,*
> *I lift this curse rest assured*

Darkness leave him, go away,
the curse is lifted now, today!"

Smitten, Battered, Beaten, Torn

This is a Voodoo spell of torment and pain affliction

Light two black candles on the altar. Take a voodoo doll and visualize it as your enemy. Place any personal items (hair, nail clippings, personal possession, photo) on the doll to imbue the victims energies. Slam the doll onto the altar and stab one time with a pin in the spot you wish to inflict pain. A second pin may also be used to inflict another area. Each time you stab the doll with a pin you will inflict pain in that area. Do not touch the pins after you have placed them, this will cause the curse to reverse back on to you. While placing the pins say:
"Smitten, battered, beaten, torn
I prick at thee as if a thorn
Suffer now I will not wait
With this pain I seal your fate
Pins so sharp and made of steel
I stick at thee, these pins you'll feel
Smitten, battered, beaten, torn
I curse you now, your pain is born!"

Lucifer's Touch

BEST TIME: Midnight

Light three black candles. Ring a bell three times then say three times:
"I call to the mighty bringer of light, Lucifer…

Spirits of the abyss, here my call
all most powerful one and all
Lucifer my thoughts do sing
through the universe they now ring
Take thine enemy, take him smite
Break him, scorn him in the night
From the mighty depths of hell
cast your darkness on his shell
Oh Lucifer, oh shinning star
Touch him, burn him from afar
Revenge now will have its day
for thine enemy starts to fray
So mote it be"

Weight Loss Spell

You will need the following items for this spell:
White Candle
Piece of paper
Plate

Go to a quiet place and write on the piece of paper how much you want to lose. Then burn the paper while Chanting:

Burn, burn, burn away,
Burn these stubborn pounds away!

Put the burning piece of paper on the plate and make sure the paper is completely burned.

Directions:
Do this spell for one week or more depending how much weight you want to lose. It will not get rid of the pounds right away but it will help you lose it faster. The spell is a lot better if you are on a diet but still good if you are not.

Attraction Love Spell

The purpose of this spell is to attract the person you love. This spell is most effective when performed during a full moon or when the moon is waxing. For this spell you will need:
• Pink candle
• Favorite perfume or essential oil
• Toothpick
Take the candle and engrave a heart into it with the toothpick. Place the candle on a windowsill with the heart in the moonlight. Place the perfume or essential oil in front of the candle and say, *"Oshun, bestow upon me the love that I need; let this scent attract (name) to me!"*
Once the candle burns out naturally, carry the perfume with you and spray little every time you go out to meet people. To intensify the strength of the spell, repeat the chant as you spray on the perfume.

Final Word

I do hope you have enjoyed this little book of spells and curses….and the lot, which all come from my private grimoire that no one has ever viewed. These spells are all spells I have had great success with, and I do hope you have great success as well.

May your life be better from the spells and information you have learned from within this book. Maybe later I will publish my full grimoire, but it is unlikely…well if this sells well I for sure will, only because I know that this has helped many people. I do not care about making any money from this, I mean it is nice but what I am doing is sharing my knowledge about magick with whomever decides to pick this book up.

Until next time…

xoxoxoxoxox,

Lady Katerina

Blessed are those who've read these pages,
Safe from harm and safe from dangers.
The witches who have read my words,
For them these words shall not be blurred.
For those full of frivolous rage,
For those who wish to engage,
And use my spells in a frivolous way
Their lives Hecate shall take away.
Their lives Kali will take away.
Kali shall slay and take away.
Hecate shall slay and take away.
Blessed are the witches who are true.
No harm to them shall come to be
By tongue pf cat and witch's brew
This here be my decree.
As I will it, so shall it be.

CPSIA information can be obtained
at www.ICGtesting.com
Printed in the USA
LVOW04s0844120218

566205LV00010B/129/P

9 781983 405969